WOMEN'S PRO BASKETBALL TODAY

THE HISTORY OF THE SACRAMENTO
# MONARCHS

ERIC BRAUN

Published by Creative Education
123 South Broad Street, Mankato, Minnesota 56001
Creative Education is an imprint of The Creative Company

Design by Stephanie Blumenthal
Cover design by Kathy Petelinsek
Production design by Andy Rustad

Photos by: NBA Photos

**Library of Congress Cataloging-in-Publication Data**

Braun, Eric 1971-
The History of the Sacramento Monarchs / by Eric Braun.
p. cm. — (Women's Pro Basketball Today)
Summary: Describes the history of the Sacramento Monarchs professional
women's basketball team and profiles some of their leading players.
ISBN 1-58341-016-3

1. Sacramento Monarchs (Basketball team) Juvenile literature. 2. Basketball for women—
United States Juvenile [1. Sacramento Monarchs (Basketball team) 2. Women basketball players.
3. Basketball players.] I. Title. II. Series.

GV885.52.S25B73  1999                                        99-18885
796.323'64'0979454—dc21                                      CIP

First Edition

2  4  6  8  9  7  5  3  1

In two years of play in Sacramento, the Monarchs of the
Women's National Basketball Association have endured just
about every problem a team can suffer. Their star, Ruthie Bolton-
Holifield has missed more than half of the Monarchs' games with
knee injuries. After a disappointing first season, Sacramento management over-hauled the roster, bringing in four players 23 years
old or younger. The team has posted a dismal 18–40 record in its
two seasons. Yet with the incredible support of their fans, the
Monarchs have survived all hardships and grown stronger. With
stars Bolton-Holifield and Bridgette Gordon supported by a
talented crop of youngsters that includes amazing guard Ticha
Penicheiro, the Monarchs are on the rise.

**MULTITALENTED**

**STAR GUARD RUTHIE**

**BOLTON-HOLIFIELD**

## LOFTY EXPECTATIONS

**W**hen the Women's National Basketball Association was still in the planning stages, few people suspected that Sacramento would be awarded a team. For the WNBA to survive, it would need to choose its cities carefully, finding sites that could provide a large, loyal fan base. Although many of the cities chosen could boast prestigious National Basketball Association teams with winning traditions and solid fan followings, the Kings—Sacramento's NBA team—could lay claim to neither of these qualities.

But in October 1996, the league announced that Sacramento would receive one of the original eight teams. WNBA officials explained that Sacramento's application simply showed more enthusiasm and energy than other cities, many of which were awarded teams based largely on their storied basketball histories. Over the next two seasons, when the Monarchs played at their highest level, it was that energy and positive attitude that would distinguish them from the rest of the league.

In January 1997, the WNBA assigned two veteran players to the Monarchs: Bridgette Gordon and Ruthie Bolton-Holifield. Gordon, a 6-foot forward, came to Sacramento with impressive credentials that included All-American honors and the 1989 NCAA championship Most Valuable Player award during her

VETERAN MONARCH BRIDGETTE GORDON

college career at Tennessee. The Florida native was also a perennial All-Star in the professional Italian League and was a member of the 1988 gold medal-winning U.S. Olympic team.

Ruthie Bolton-Holifield—or "Mighty Ruthie," as she is known—was a starting guard on the 1996 U.S. Olympic team that went 60–0 and captured gold in the Summer Games. The explosive and multitalented Bolton-Holifield took her skills to Sweden, Hungary, Italy, and Turkey before returning to her native country. Although the Monarchs still had no coach or completed roster yet, two cornerstones had been set into place. Sacramento fans, sensing a winner, lined up to buy season tickets.

Mary Murphy, a basketball mind with an energetic and charismatic reputation, was soon named the first head coach of the Monarchs. Murphy came to California after leading the University of Wisconsin to a 20–9 record and a NCAA tournament berth in 1992, accomplishments that earned her Big Ten Coach of the Year honors.

As the team's first training camp approached, Sacramento continued to develop its roster. In the league's Elite Draft on February 27, 1997, the Monarchs added power forward Judy Mosley-McAfee. They also picked up Mikiko Hagiwara, a sharp-shooting guard from Japan, to add to the team's offensive versatility.

Two months later, Sacramento brought its 1997 starting lineup into focus when it drafted forward Pam McGee and guard Chantel Tremitiere. Team officials hoped that the 6-foot-3 McGee, who had played professional basketball around the

world for nine years, would pair with Gordon to provide a strong veteran frontcourt. The 5-foot-6 Tremitiere, meanwhile, appeared to be a fine complement to Bolton-Holifield, as both players were capable of scoring, creating plays, and applying tough defensive pressure.

From the beginning of her tenure, the confident Murphy gave voice to the building enthusiasm of fans and team officials. "Our goal is to win a championship," the determined coach said before the season. "Why the heck not?"

Coach Murphy wasted no time in establishing a sense of teamwork among her players. When training camp opened on May 28 at ARCO Arena, Murphy gathered her players together at mid-court. "We've got to take care of our bodies, our minds, and our souls," she said. "And we've got to take care of each other. That's what's going to set us apart."

## HIGH HOPES

The league's first game was a much-hyped, televised matchup between two high-profile teams: the New York Liberty and the Los Angeles Sparks. Players from both teams looked nervous in a sloppy contest. After watching the game on television, Monarchs forward Bridgette Gordon had a talk with her team. She told them to relax and to not let the pressure get to them in their opening

FIRST-ROUND DRAFT PICK

TICHA PENICHEIRO (ABOVE);

FORWARD LINDA

BURGESS (LEFT)

1998 ROOKIE TANGELA SMITH

game against the Utah Starzz. "I told them to just go out there and play," Gordon said.

The Monarchs did play, setting aside all pre-game jitters. In front of 8,915 pumped-up Utah fans, including Utah Jazz stars Karl Malone and John Stockton, the Monarchs jumped out to a quick lead. Bolton-Holifield's sterling defense helped keep the Starzz at bay, and Sacramento went into the half with a seven-point lead.

The closest Utah got in the second half was 46–40 with 12:39 left to play. But the gap quickly widened as Gordon collected seven straight points and Judy Mosley-McAfee added four on an 11–0 run that put the game out of reach. The Monarchs hung on to win their first game 70–60.

Two days later, 15,259 fans turned out to watch Sacramento's first regular-season home game. The rowdy crowd greeted their team with a standing ovation, but they would find little to cheer about after that as the New York Liberty overwhelmed the Monarchs. New York cruised to a 39–24 halftime lead and then stretched the margin to 57–34 with less than 10 minutes left on the clock.

Desperate to turn things around, Coach Murphy called a timeout. When her disheartened team reached the bench, she

SACRAMENTO PLAYED WITH

ENTHUSIASM EARLY (ABOVE);

DANIELLE VIGLIONE

(BELOW)

**NAME:** Ruthie Bolton-Holifield

**BORN:** May 27, 1967 (Lucedale, Miss.)

**POSITION:** Guard

**HEIGHT:** 5-foot-9

**COLLEGE:** Auburn '89

**AWARDS AND HONORS:** All-WNBA First Team 1997, Player of the Week 6-21-97

Bolton-Holifield thrived in the league in 1997, finishing second in league scoring, fifth in steals, and 10th in rebounds. Bolton-Holifield led the Monarchs in scoring 17 times and twice finished with a career-high 34 points. She missed five games due to a strained knee in '97, but her luck was much worse the following season. After only five games in 1998, she tore her left anterior cruciate ligament and missed the remainder of the schedule, leaving a gaping hole in the Monarch lineup.

**STATISTICS:** 502 career points

| Year | Average | Total Points | Avg. Rebounds |
|------|---------|--------------|---------------|
| 1997 | 19.4 | 447 | 5.8 |
| 1998 | 11 | 55 | 2.2 |

12

**NAME:** Latasha Byears

**BORN:** August 12, 1973 (Memphis, Tenn.)

**POSITION:** Forward

**HEIGHT:** 5-foot-11

**COLLEGE:** DePaul '96

Originally assigned to the developmental squad, Byears was activated by Sacramento on June 20, 1997, and went on to be Sacramento's leading scorer the following season. As a rookie in '97, she notched 11 double-doubles and set her single-game record with 17 rebounds in back-to-back games in late July. In 1998 Byears led Sacramento in rebounding for the second straight year, finishing ninth in league average. Her scoring average was eighth-best in the WNBA and tops for the Monarchs, and her 28 points against Phoenix was a personal best.

**STATISTICS:** 671 career points

| Year | Average | Total Points | Avg. Rebounds |
|------|---------|--------------|---------------|
| 1997 | 8.7     | 244          | 6.9           |
| 1998 | 14.2    | 427          | 6.6           |

motioned to the fans and barked at her players, "You'd better do something to make these people want to come back, because right now you're not doing a whole lot."

Her words must have struck a chord. The Monarchs burst back into the game, cutting the margin to 70–62. In the end, however, Sacramento ran out of time. "We were just too hyped up," said Bolton-Holifield, who scored 27 points and grabbed 12 rebounds. "We were too emotional." Although the Monarchs lost their home opener by the score of 73–62, they proved that they could play with the WNBA's best teams.

After one week of play, the Monarchs were 2–2, and "Mighty Ruthie" was named the WNBA's first Player of the Week. The intense guard averaged a league-leading 21.5 points in the first four games, along with 8.5 rebounds, 3.5 assists, and 2.8 steals. Bolton-Holifield and the other team veterans were providing the leadership and points that had been expected of them, and the younger players were learning quickly. The next month, however, would be a dark one for the young franchise.

## TURMOIL AND CHANGE

On July 12, 1997, in the midst of a humiliating 28-point loss to the Houston Comets, Ruthie Bolton-Holifield crumpled to the floor in pain. She had strained her left knee and

RESERVE GUARD FRANTHEA PRICE

would miss five games. The rest of the Monarchs would have to step up their games if Sacramento was to compete without the league's top scorer.

In their next game, the Monarchs showed that they could. With the score close between the Monarchs and the Los Angeles Sparks late in the second half, young reserve forward Latasha Byears took over. With 2:37 remaining, she threw a perfect lob pass to Pam McGee, giving the Monarchs a 70–68 lead. Moments later, a Byears steal led to a fast-break layup by guard Chantel Tremitiere. Then, after the Sparks closed the lead to three, Byears found a lane through the L.A. defense for a layup with the shot clock winding down.

When the final buzzer sounded, Byears had scored 21 points and pulled down 10 rebounds in her first professional start, and Sacramento had a 78–73 win. "I'm always ready to step up to the task," Byears said after the game. "I mean, that's why I'm here. To play basketball." Fans may not have known it then, but they had witnessed the birth of a new WNBA star. Soon, as the Monarchs' season would fall apart, the emergence of Byears would prove to be a much-needed bright spot.

Early in the nine-game losing skid that followed, it was obvious that something had to change. Coach Murphy waived

guard-forward Corissa Yasen and benched guard Mikiko Hagiwara before a 60–82 home loss against Houston. She then cut power forward Judy Mosley-McAfee and contacted several teams in an effort to trade inconsistent center Pamela McGee.

When Mighty Ruthie returned on July 27, Murphy put McGee back in the lineup to try to shake things up and keep the team's playoff hopes from slipping away entirely. Unfortunately, Ruthie came back cold, sinking just 6 of 21 shots in a 62–84 home loss to the L.A. Sparks—the Monarchs' fifth loss in a row.

Monarchs owner Jim Thomas had seen enough: a 5–10 record, a five-game losing streak, and growing player discontent required a drastic change. The next day, Mary Murphy was fired, and assistant coach Heidi VanDerveer was promoted in her place. Yvette Angel, a guard who had been cut from the Monarchs' roster the day before, was brought back as the assistant coach.

The players seemed pleased with the change. "Heidi is very motivational," Bolton-Holifield said. "She's very positive." With new leadership, the Monarchs were ready to put the weeks of injuries, drastic roster changes, and uninspired play behind them. They decided that their remaining schedule would be a whole new season.

ADIA BARNES (ABOVE);

FORWARD LINDA

BURGESS (BELOW)

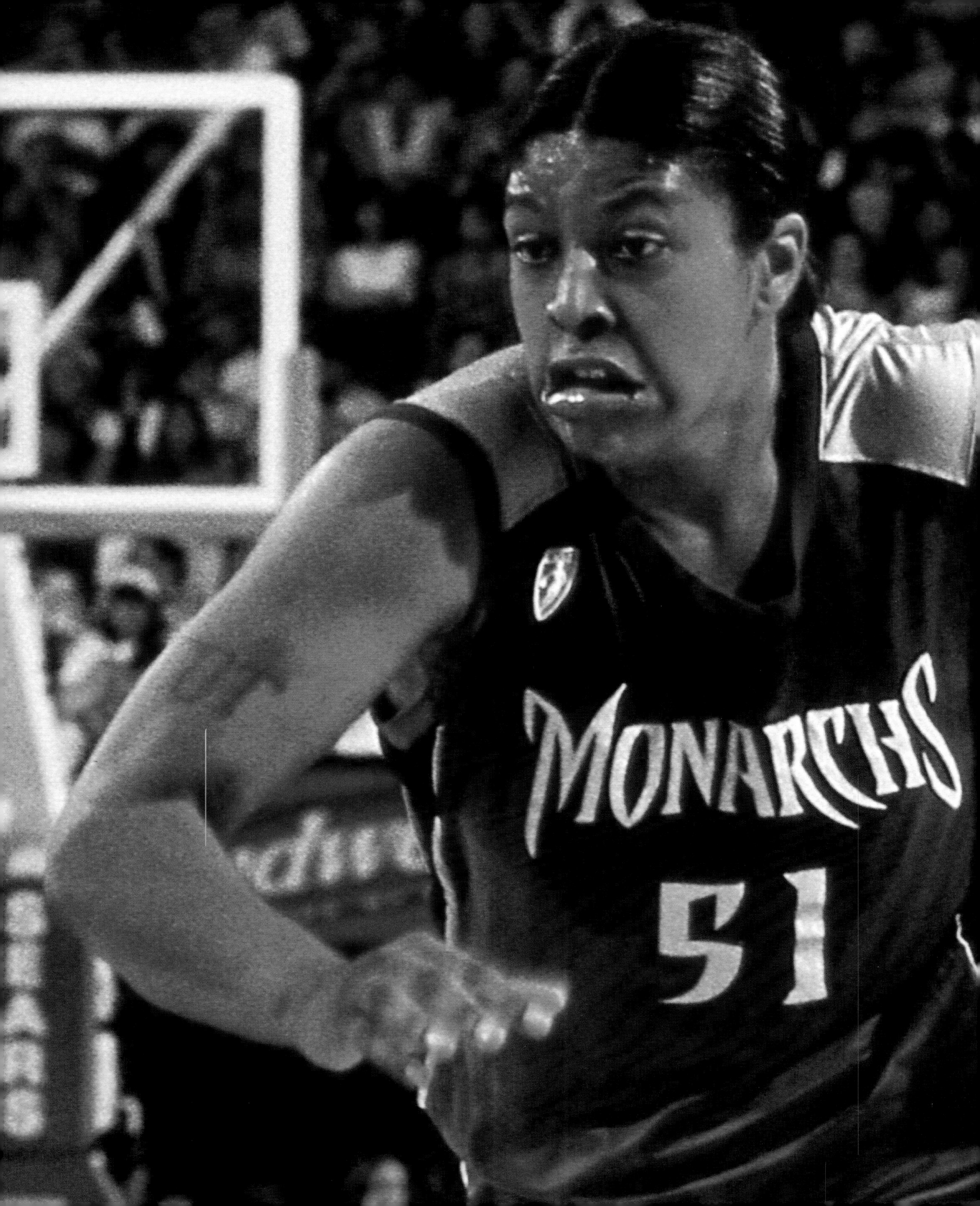
MONARCHS
51

## A NEW ATTITUDE

**W**ith VanDerveer at the helm, the Monarchs lost their next four games in a row, bringing their total losing streak to nine. But the team was beginning to jell.

One of those losses came in overtime against the powerhouse New York Liberty, a game the Monarchs felt they could have won. When they played the Liberty 11 days later, this time in Sacramento's ARCO Arena, they did win. Byears, matched up against Liberty star Rebecca Lobo, led the way with 23 points and eight rebounds and limited Lobo to a mere two points. "We've got a new attitude," said Gordon, who scored 19 points. "We're playing with pride."

Two nights later, Mighty Ruthie racked up a mammoth 34 points on six-of-nine three-point shooting as the Monarchs defeated the Cleveland Rockers 81–76 for their fourth win in a row. Even the Rockers had to admit that the Monarchs were a changed team. "I think Sacramento may have found their chemistry and their rhythm," said Cleveland guard Michelle Edwards. "Before, when we played them, they were just totally out of sync. But that's all built with time, and it's their time now."

The drastic difference seemed to be the result of Coach VanDerveer's new team rule: have fun. "When you're lucky enough to play basketball for a living, you should have fun," VanDerveer said. "We still want them to focus on doing their jobs, but let's face it, this is a game. It should be a pleasure to play."

After Sacramento's nightmarish nine-game losing streak, the playoffs were no more than a dream, but the fans didn't seem to care. Their team was playing with heart every night. When someone made a critical shot or a fancy pass, the squad on the court would high-five while the bench players came to their feet, whooping and swinging towels.

More than 10,000 fans showed up for the Monarchs' last home game of the season, a 69–54 loss to the Phoenix Mercury. Despite the losing finale to a sub-par season, the crowd didn't want to go home. So the Monarchs threw jerseys and shoes in the stands. Still, the crowd cheered for more. "Tonight, after the game," Coach VanDerveer said, "you couldn't help but be excited for the future of this club and the city."

## QUICK, BIG, AND UNPREDICTABLE

The Monarchs posted a 5–8 record under VanDerveer, but the coach had very few critics. Her team played better after her appointment, and morale went through the roof. Attendance, which had dipped during the losing streak, was back up by the end of the season. However, VanDerveer knew that she would have to improve her roster in the off-season if the Monarchs expected to compete for the playoffs in 1998. Having a strong draft would be critical.

FOURTH-ROUND

DRAFT PICK

ADIA BARNES

**NAME:** Ticha Penicheiro

**BORN:** September 18, 1974 (Figueira da Fox, Portugal)

**POSITION:** Guard

**HEIGHT:** 5-foot-11

**COLLEGE:** Old Dominion '98

Selected second in the 1998 draft, Penicheiro dazzled the league with her passing. As a rookie, she led the WNBA in assists and minutes per game and finished fourth in steals without missing a start in 30 games. Her 16 assists against Cleveland on July 29th set a WNBA single-game record. Other season highlights included a 13-point, 13-assist performance against Washington and a 14-point, 12-assist night in a win over Charlotte. Penicheiro's court instincts and intelligent play promise to entertain WNBA crowds for years to come.

**STATISTICS:** 190 career points

| Year | Average | Total Points | Avg. Assists |
|------|---------|--------------|--------------|
| 1998 | 6.3 | 190 | 7.5 |

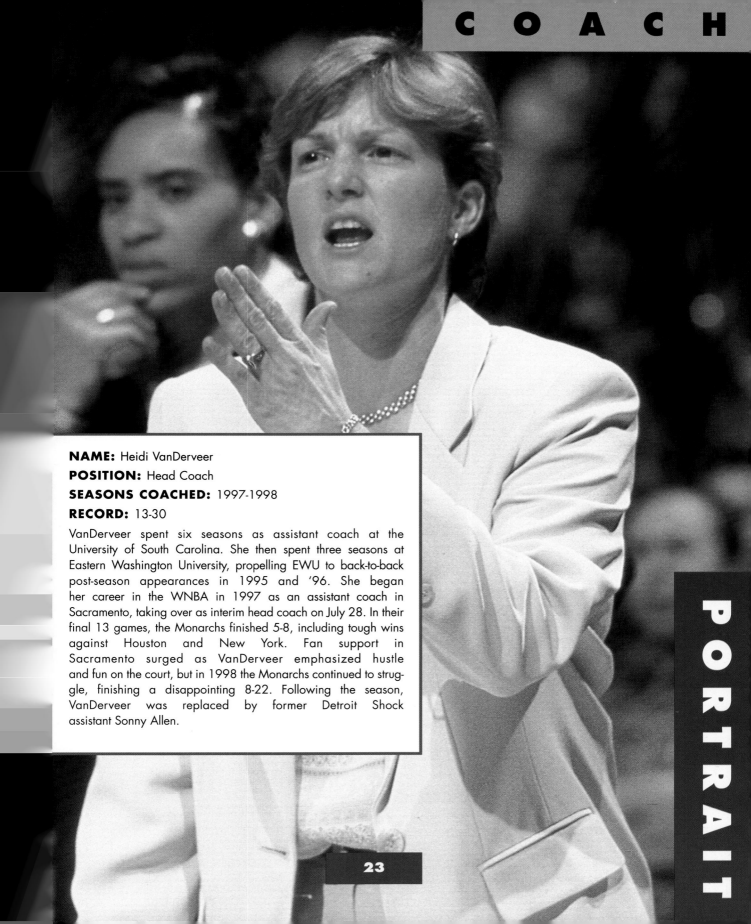

**NAME:** Heidi VanDerveer

**POSITION:** Head Coach

**SEASONS COACHED:** 1997-1998

**RECORD:** 13-30

VanDerveer spent six seasons as assistant coach at the University of South Carolina. She then spent three seasons at Eastern Washington University, propelling EWU to back-to-back post-season appearances in 1995 and '96. She began her career in the WNBA in 1997 as an assistant coach in Sacramento, taking over as interim head coach on July 28. In their final 13 games, the Monarchs finished 5-8, including tough wins against Houston and New York. Fan support in Sacramento surged as VanDerveer emphasized hustle and fun on the court, but in 1998 the Monarchs continued to struggle, finishing a disappointing 8-22. Following the season, VanDerveer was replaced by former Detroit Shock assistant Sonny Allen.

With her first selection in the 1998 WNBA Draft, Van-Derveer chose point guard Ticha Penicheiro, a two-time All-American out of Old Dominion. Penicheiro was known as an intelligent player with keen court instincts and a flair for flashy passes. After finding her starter at the point, VanDerveer used the team's remaining picks to acquire forwards Tangela Smith and Adia Barnes and 6-foot-5 center Quacy Barnes.

The 6-foot-4 Smith, who had just earned Big Ten Player of the Year honors at Iowa, gave the Monarchs a scorer, rebounder, and exceptional shot-blocker. Coach VanDerveer knew that Adia Barnes, who had just graduated from the University of Arizona as the school's all-time leader in rebounds and steals, also had star potential at the WNBA level.

After adding to her team through the draft, VanDerveer continued to re-shape the roster with off-season moves. She traded former starters Pamela McGee and Chantel Tremitiere for forward-center Linda Burgess and guard Lady Hardmon. She also picked up free agents Franthea Price and Tiffani Johnson.

The Monarchs were quicker, bigger (with four players 6-foot-3 or taller), and more athletic than they had been during the 1997 season. They were also younger—with an average age of less than 26 years old—which added a dimension of unpredictability to the club. "Because of our energy, right off the bat we should be able to beat some people we aren't expected to beat," VanDerveer said. "With our inexperience, we will probably lose a couple of games we'll have a chance to win."

Monarchs fans had good reason to be optimistic about their new-look team. The backcourt of Penicheiro and Bolton-Holifield promised to be one of the best in the league. Sacramento management could also count on veterans Bolton-Holifield and Gordon to guide the younger Monarchs into their first WNBA season. With their first four games coming at home, the Monarchs hoped to get off to a quick start.

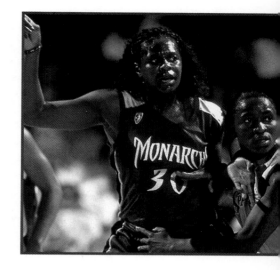

OFFENSIVE THREAT

BRIDGETTE GORDON

(ABOVE); ADIA BARNES

(BELOW)

## REFLECTIONS OF '97

After dropping their 1998 opener to Phoenix, the Monarchs bounced back to beat the L.A. Sparks 73–69. Sacramento was down by five with just 4:37 left to play when Latasha Byears took control. She nailed a 10-foot jumper to cut the lead to three, and her fast-break layup with 1:36 left gave the Monarchs a 66–64 lead and set the stage for a wild finish.

Sparks forward Lisa Leslie scored and hit a free throw, giving the one-point edge back to L.A. with 1:05 to go. But on the ensuing Monarchs possession, Byears attacked the glass, tearing a rebound away from Leslie and converting the shot while being fouled. She added the free throw to give Sacramento a 69–67 lead. With 35 seconds left, Bolton-Holifield made a critical steal, sealing the victory.

The team was playing with confidence, but on June 23 they would see their season wither away in a single moment. Playing against the expansion Detroit Shock, Bolton-Holifield drove to the basket, pulled up for a shot, and tumbled to the floor. Players and fans immediately thought of the star's injury the previous season, but this time it was worse. Bolton-Holifield had torn the anterior cruciate ligament in her left knee and would miss the rest of the season's 25 games.

By early July, with the Monarchs at 3–8, it became clear that they desperately needed more experience and proven leadership in the lineup. Without Bolton-Holifield, Gordon and Burgess were the only true veterans still active. On July 6, the Monarchs traded 22-year-old center Tiffani Johnson to Phoenix for 30-year-old center Pauline Jordan. Jordan, a 6-foot-3 inside player, brought eight years of professional European playing experience to the Monarchs.

TRADED TO THE MONARCHS,

LINDA BURGESS (ABOVE);

AND LADY HARDMON

(BELOW)

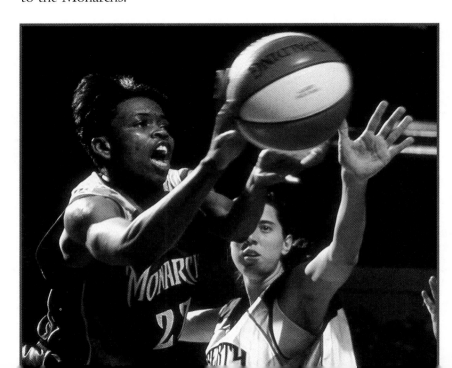

Although victories didn't come any easier after the trade, the younger players did respond with inspired play. In the week following the trade, Ticha Penicheiro averaged 10 assists per game. Tangela Smith found her game too, scoring a career-high 20 points in 24 minutes against Los Angeles and setting a franchise record with five blocked shots against Charlotte soon after.

Byears, meanwhile, continued to establish herself as the team's "go-to" player. Over the next five games in mid-July, she averaged 18.4 points and 8.6 rebounds per contest, including a career-high 28 points against Phoenix. The 5-foot-11 Byears, who had become the Monarchs' primary scorer despite her relatively small size at the forward position, never believed that her height was a restriction. "It's the size of your heart that counts," she explained.

As different players led the Monarchs from night to night, Bolton-Holifield watched from the bench as her team struggled for wins. "The hardest part of all this is feeling that I let the team down," she said.

On August 15, the Monarchs unleashed their unpredictable side, routing the Utah Starzz 82–55. They outscored Utah by an incredible 35 points in the second half, due in large part to Penicheiro's 14 rebounds. "I think that she is the best point guard in the league," Utah coach Frank Layden said after Penicheiro shredded his Starzz. The Monarchs were young, but they had heart.

FREE AGENTS
FRANTHEA PRICE (ABOVE);
AND TIFFANI JOHNSON
(BELOW)

SACRAMENTO FANS SHOWED

THEIR SUPPORT (ABOVE);

DANIELLE VIGLIONE

(BELOW)

## MONARCHS ON THE RISE

The Monarchs' last home game of the year came against Phoenix, who was on its way to the WNBA playoffs for the second year in a row. Sacramento started strong early, jumping out to an 18–14 lead. However, Phoenix fired right back, taking control with a 16–3 run. The Monarchs were never close again, losing 85–69. "Our youth really showed down the stretch," admitted Adia Barnes, who did her best for Sacramento by drilling three of four shots from beyond the three-point arc.

As it did the previous year, the Sacramento crowd stuck around after the final game to thank the players for their efforts with a long standing ovation. After players gave away autographed jerseys, gave short speeches, and finally left the floor, the fans were still screaming. The surprising show of support after a disastrous season left Coach VanDerveer and her players a little misty-eyed. "These are true fans," Penicheiro said.

The survival of the WNBA depends on fans around the country. Nowhere was this tested more than in Sacramento, where fans watched their team struggle mightily in both its seasons. The Monarchs finished the 1998 season with an 8–22 record—two losses worse than they had in 1997. They averaged 63.9 points per game and made only .260 of their three-point shots, both league

TICHA PENICHEIRO'S PASSING DAZZLED THE LEAGUE.

lows. The team also finished near the bottom of the league standings in shooting percentage from the floor and the free-throw line.

Yet despite the poor numbers, the Monarchs certainly gave their fans a good show. Watching the rookies develop was a pleasure for any true basketball fan. Tangela Smith emerged as a dominant shot-blocker, excellent shooter, and exceptional all-around athlete. Adia Barnes was terrific off the bench, proving herself as an aggressive player with a knack for three-pointers.

And then there was Penicheiro, with her crowd-pleasing passes. She tossed no-look passes, over-the-shoulder flips, wraparounds, court-length one-bouncers, shovel passes, and tip passes, frequently drawing gasps and applause from the Sacramento faithful. She alone was a good enough reason for many fans to come out to ARCO Arena.

Monarchs fans, players, and management are all confident that the Monarchs will soon rise among the league's championship contenders. The 1998 rookies are older and wiser, and Bolton-Holifield is expected to return with a vengeance. After a relatively stable off-season free of the previous year's personnel changes, the Monarchs finally seem to have the team unity that had been lacking.

After assembling perhaps the best rookie class of the 1998 draft, Sacramento is ready for the future. Ticha Penicheiro, Tangela Smith, and Adia Barnes, the standouts of this young squad, have formed a strong nucleus. This youthfulness, together with the team's veteran experience and the return of Mighty Ruthie, should make the Monarchs one of the league's most exciting—and dangerous—teams for years to come.